Me
in Relationship to
You

Me
in Relationship to
You

Reflections on Love, Loss, and a Life Well-lived

To Carrie

Poetry and Prose

2/15/22

Mac McShane, Psy.D

Mac McShane

Sopris Mountain Press
Carbondale, Colorado 2021

Me in Relationship to You
Reflections on Love, Loss, and a Life Well-lived

Copyright© 2021 by Dr. Mac McShane

All rights reserved. Published in the United States by
Sopris Mountain Press, Carbondale, Colorado

"A Friendship Blessing" from Anam Cara by John O'Donohue.
Copyright (c) 1997 by John O'Donohue.
Used by permission of HarperCollins Publishers.

For information about permission to reproduce selections
from this book, write to macm@prodigy.net

Print ISBN: 978-1-7369357-0-5
EISBN: 978-1-7369357-1-2

Library of Congress Control Number: 2021907403

Me in Relationship to You™ is a Sopris Mountain Press, trademark.

Names: McShane, Mac, author.
Title: Me in Relationship to You
Reflections on Love, Loss, and a Life Well-lived
Description: Carbondale, Colorado: Sopris Mountain Press, 2021
Identifiers: ISBN 978-1-7369357-0-5 (print) | ISBN 978-1-7369357-1-2 (ebook)

Cover and Interior Design: Cindi Yaklich Epicenter Creative, LLC

In Loving Memory of Benjamin Hirsch-McShane
April 19, 1983 – January 25, 2019

Ben, you are my son in this life, my soul mate forever

Contents

PART THREE: Finding Our Way

We're dealing with the subject of human sense making.
How people are in the world and how they make sense of
the world. That's sacred work.

Robert Kegan – *The Art of Developmental Coaching*

A Friendship Blessing – by John O'Donohue

May you be blessed with good friends.
May you learn to be a good friend yourself.
May you be able to journey to that place in your soul where
there is great love, warmth, feeling and forgiveness.
May this change you.
May it transfigure that which is negative, distant, or cold
in you.
May you be brought into the real passion, kinship, and
affinity of belonging.
May you treasure your friends.
May you be good to them and may you be there for them;
may they bring you all the blessings, challenges, truth,
and light that you need for your journey.
May you never be isolated.
May you always be in the gentle nest of belonging with your
anam ċara.

Anam is the Celtic word for soul. *Ċara* is the word for friend. So *anam ċara* means
soul friend. The *anam ċara* was a person to whom you could reveal the hidden
intimacies of your life. The friendship was an act of recognition and belonging.
When you had an anam ċara, your friendship cut across all convention and category.
You were joined in an ancient and eternal way with the friend of your soul.

John O'Donohue from the book, *Anam Ċara: A Book of Celtic Wisdom*

You Know That Guy

Written by Rahul, a friend of Ben's, Sunday, Feb 3, 2019 at 3:33 AM.

(Rahul had posted this online. He is one of many close friends of Ben who I had never really even known before Ben's death.)

"You know, that one guy who goes to your bachelor party even though he doesn't know anyone else and gets along with, nay charms everyone there. People are talking about hanging out with him with their spouses when they get back home and thanking him for bringing all his energy to the weekend.

You know, that dude who when you get to your shitty new job after moving across the country alone is immediately your best bud and takes you out to all the hip spots in town.

You know, that broseph who you immediately connect with because you have the same sense of humor and he's super easygoing. You guys can spend all day talking about your hump of a boss and how much better life would be if people just focused on being happy instead of money, friends instead of things, family instead of status.

You know, that smarty pants who gets in and goes to UPenn but gets tired of all the poseurs his freshman year and goes back home so he can be closer to the people and the mountains he loves.

You know, that kid whose parents are all therapists, so he's about the best listener ever and his advice is good, not preachy. He's got empathy at a time when so few do.

You know, that man of mystery who you feel like is one of your best friends, but at the same time has so many true best friends that you've never even met. How's he even have the time for so many deep and powerful and lasting connections?

You know, the *dhoniyo* who becomes so at ease in your home country of India that it becomes clear he's way more comfortable there than you ever will be. He knows the people, the culture, the traditions – he's been adopted.

You know, that homey that keeps it so real with you that they are willing to tell you that maybe getting married to your first wife is a bad idea and when you ignore the advice, he isn't judgey; you guys just order another beer. *C'est la vie.*

You know, that suave cat who introduces you to his girlfriends and they are all so different but all so great. And they love him for his sensitivity, not his machismo. And you think, how's this guy pulling it off without being a dick?

You know, that chill friend who is out of town when you go to SF but leaves you his door code, keys and a fresh set of sheets so you and your girl can stay at their place.

You know, that bud who calls to tell you that he's met Sarah, the love of his life and he's gonna marry her and tells you about how she knew he had the ring for her for like a year while they traveled the world together and never once pressed him on when he was gonna pop the question. Never even told him that she knew about it.

You know, that amigo who invites you and your girlfriend to his wedding in Tulum and you're just in awe of all of their friends and family. The sheer joy. You remember the details and 12 months later when you get married to Karin, you plan your wedding to be just like theirs and are so happy you did because the focus is on love, friends, and family and nothing else.

You know? You know. I know this man.

That's Ben Hirsch-McShane.

Maybe it's a cop-out but I do prefer to think that when people leave us, they are just on a long adventure to some far out wilderness where they don't get cell service. Is there any doubt that when we see Ben again, he's gonna have the best goddamn stories about what he's been doing since he went on this trip?

We will all miss you, Benihana."

Introduction

My last outing with my son Ben was skinning up Tiehack Ski Area outside of Aspen on a bluebird Colorado day in January 2019. For anyone unfamiliar with the term "skinning up," it refers to using climbing skins on your backcountry skis to walk up the mountain before taking them off to ski down. Ben was out visiting, combining work in Denver with a visit to my wife's and my home in the Aspen area to play before he headed off on a back country hut trip in Montana with friends. He was excited to try out his new backcountry ski gear before his trip.

Even though it was the end of January, we were down to our tee shirts and still sweating. Climbing and talking about our lives, joyful that we still made it a priority to spend time together to do things we loved in beautiful, natural places. We had marveled throughout our three days together at the parallels in our lives as well as our shared curiosity about finding meaning in our lives and understanding what it meant to have a life well-lived.

Although Cynthia, my wife and Ben's second mom, was not with us that day, the three of us had been spending a magical three days together skiing powder, cooking and eating, drinking great red wine, and talking late into the night about our lives, our dreams and our fears. I had been a primary caretaker of Ben his whole life, which had created an amazing connection between the two of us as well as with Cynthia, his stepmother since he was three years old. As with all relationships, there had been ups and downs. Now with Ben at 35 and a successful hedge fund manager living in San Francisco, the three of us could more easily celebrate the connections we had forged over the years. All of us were proud of each other and happy to share our successes, our fears, and our new goals focused on learning and growing in that ongoing quest to become our better selves. We had no way of knowing that within the week Ben would be dead — killed in a backcountry avalanche in western Montana.

I don't know if you have ever lost someone at the center of your life — someone you had never even considered could leave this world with you still here? I know that I never had before this overwhelming tragic loss of my son, Ben. Even though Ben and I had talked about that very concept (and yes, it was only a concept then, I know now) just six days before he died. As I wrote in my journal just after his death: "but I was talking about my mortality, Ben, not yours." Both of my parents had died in the prior five years, so I was well-practiced in death and grieving, or so I thought. Yet they were in their 90's with failing systems and ready to let go. That is part of how we all avoid thinking about death, it is something that happens to others: old people, people who live in war zones far away, people with pre-existing conditions, or those who did not take good care of themselves or . . .

Yes, my tidy little view of the world held the concept of death, my taking leave of Ben, others maybe dying for "reasons that made sense," anything to keep me from considering that my only son could die and the mere conscious thought of that would have made me too scared to sleep. My view of life and death was not large enough or wildly frightening enough to hold even the possibility of my son's dying before me. Yes, everyone dies. That concept, I, we, you accept in the abstract. What makes the death of a child, your child, such the draconian nightmare is that this brutal reality can suddenly become real in your own life, in that gut wrenching way that stark, cold facts sometimes become real. Instantaneously, without warning or time to prepare, your only child is dead. Simply, finally dead, gone from your life, extinguished from this world with no recourse, no bargaining, or final goodbye. Friends come to comfort you, cry with you, cook for you, and make sure you are not alone. They are in shock as much as you even as they try to hide their terror from you. No one knows what to say and, for now, that is just as well. We find shelter in being able to do something, anything that can connect us to the lives we imagined we had just hours ago.

My wife and I both have doctorates in clinical psychology and have been therapists and executive coaches for many years. We know something about loss and healing, death and grieving, and traumatic events. Yet, that, for the most part, does not help absorb our own grief. We know that there is no one right way to grieve and that each person has to find his or her own way. We know the only wrong way to grieve is to lock the feelings up too tightly inside and let them fester for too long. It is best to have friends and family who support you as you all flail around and get run over again and again by thoughts and feelings that you have no place to gently stack out of the way. We need to learn to be gentle with ourselves and yet give ourselves room to act or not act like we, and/or others, might think we should. Tragedy is the ultimate permission giver to step outside ourselves and who we think we need to be. Suddenly, we don't know who we are or why we are even still here in this world or if we want to be in a place so malicious and unkind.

The day after my son died, I started a new journal since writing is a source of solace for me, a place to go to reflect and try to make sense of my world. I started all my entries with "Dear Ben." It was a way to have a dialogue with myself and with Ben, the person I most wanted to talk with about this overwhelming event in my life.

At first, I left the facing page blank. I then started adding quotes from my emails to others, quotes from what I was reading, quotes from what others wrote to me in their notes and emails. One of the few sources of comfort I found was the writing of John O'Donohue, the Celtic philosopher and poet. My sister gave me the complete set of recordings of his work put out by Tami Simons at Sounds True, a favorite company of mine, dedicated to disseminating the spiritual wisdom of the world. Not surprisingly, I started writing on those blank pages notes and poems and blessings of John O'Donohue. By April, I had started to write my own poetry on those pages as well, something I had never done before. I was not sure where they came from or even if they were poems in any true sense of that word.

As you will see, I was trying my best to make sense of Ben's death in my writing. While I consider myself to be a very spiritual person, I did not have a very good relationship with organized religion growing up and have found traditional religious practices less helpful for me. Still, Ben's death has challenged me to continue to grow and develop and search for meaning just as we had together in our individual lives and our shared connections. I believe as many do that our society is at a crossroads. There is a tremendous energy in the world about developing ourselves and growing our conscious awareness. This is manifested in all the new materials and programs focused on meditation, mindfulness, and becoming our better selves. At the same time, there is also more anger, hatred, and division than I have witnessed before. If we are to survive, we must accelerate our growth rather than sink into division and conflict. I hope that this book of poetry can play some small part in moving us in that direction while at the same time bringing each of you who read it some solace and positive energy in your lives.

Maybe you have this book in your hand because someone gave it to you to help you deal with your own traumatic losses. I know I looked for books that could help and people gave me many books they thought would be helpful to me in my time of grief. Most did not, at least not at first. We need to find our own way. What helps me may seem weird to you. I don't know what you are feeling or needing, no one does. I can only talk about my journey thus far and share some of my writing that resonated for me. Maybe you picked this book up because the poetry is less about death and dying than learning and growing. I share this poetry with you here since it has brought me a sense of solace in a wobbly time. Very uncharacteristically of me, I had started to share it with others, beginning with my wife and then my close friends. I was surprised that they were moved by what they read and asked if I would send them copies. Several hoped that I would put my poetry together in a book to make it easier to share, reread and give to others. Thus this book was born.

The poetry that follows is divided into three sections. The first is more about the shock and early sense of being overwhelmed and trying to figure out some way to deal with what just happened. The second section is about moving from shock to trying to make some meaning about death and dying, finding reason for hope. The third and final section is about finding our way. How do we use challenges in our lives to push us to start growing and developing again in spite of or because of the losses we have experienced? How do we work to create a bigger version of ourselves? Who will we become? Why are we even here?

part one

Death Is Disruptive

The best thing for being sad, replied Merlyn, beginning to puff and blow, is to learn something. That is the only thing that never fails. You may grow old and trembling in your anatomies, you may lie awake at night listening to the disorder in your veins, you may miss your only love, you may see the world about you devastated by evil lunatics, or know your honor trampled in the sewer of baser minds. There is only one thing for it then – to learn. Learn why the world wags and what wags it.

T. H. White - *The Once and Future King*

Dealing with the Trauma and Grief of Unimaginable Loss

"Dear Ben,

Sarah called when we were skiing yesterday. The connection was bad. I think I heard her say 'Avalanche and I'm sorry, Ben has passed.' Oh God, please tell me it's not true! But Sarah doesn't call, so something is wrong. It can't be. Please . . .

You of all people, the one to be here for everyone else . . . We just had one of the greatest weekends together talking late into the night, skiing and skinning up Tiehack on your new gear. God, it can't be. I have no place in my brain or heart to hear this message. I have never once thought that I could be alive and you not be. I often think when I write in my journal that one day you might be the one to read some of my entries, after I was gone. Me not you!

My heart is broken open today, I can't breathe. Yet, everything is exactly as it was last night. I know now you were dead then too, but I had no idea. I always thought if something happened to you, I would just know. I didn't.

Ben, I am not sure what life will be like without you in my

world. I knew our time together was limited. I thought one day it might be less so, but there are many people in your life who love you. I was always so thrilled when I discovered we would have some time together. I was joyful when hearing you say how special our relationship was to you; it was for me as well. I don't know how to grieve well. The sadness inside of me may destroy me . . . . . This can't be real . . . .

Dear Ben . . . where are you? What does this even mean? . . ."

**

So started my journal entries for the next year and beyond. The journal where at first, I went to remind myself that this was still real and not a really bad dream. Later, where I went to make sense, take notes on what others had to say about life and death. And, still later, it was where I began to the write the poetry that is this book.

Over a year later, I still have good and bad days, good and bad moments. I can't tell you how you need to deal with the trauma and loss in your life. You need to give yourself permission to grieve in your own way, even if you don't yet know what your way is. Don't let others tell you what is right or what you should or shouldn't do. Trust yourself and experiment. When in doubt, try small experiments and watch the results. I knew for me I needed to write, I needed time alone, as well time and ways to share with others. I wrote long email responses to both old friends and people I barely knew. I returned to leading an intense leadership program before anyone else thought that was a good idea. I got back on skis, skiing powder alone against most everyone's best advice. It was harder than I thought and just what I needed to do. Cynthia grieved differently, and we supported each other and gave each other room, even as we worried about both ourselves and each other.

I realized early on that not only is this kind of loss incredibly difficult for those of us experiencing it, but also it is incredibly difficult for our friends and colleagues. We could use some advice on how to support our grieving friends and family members. One of the biggest worries, is "what do I say?" "What is the right thing to say?" I now know, looking back on my dealing with the grief of my friends, I had not handled it well at all. Not knowing what to say after the initial condolences and tears together, I mostly waited for them to bring it up and said nothing. Previously, I had avoided talking about what my son was doing when around a friend who had lost a child, particularly if they were close in age. When terrified by the enormity of what they experienced, I unwittingly moved a step back.

What might help us when we are trying to console others are a few guidelines. One, there is nothing really good that you can say, so relax. Avoid the platitudes that emphasize the unimaginable hurt and sorrow or the reassurance that everything happens for a reason and will be okay. Keep your religious assurances to yourself. Even if I happened to believe as you do, I am likely questioning those beliefs right now. If I don't believe as you do, it's worse. Two, I probably don't know how I am feeling or doing. Try not to ask the knee jerk questions "how are you doing?" or "are you okay?" I don't know how I'm doing but I am sure it is not okay. Three, it's okay to state the obvious as in "I heard about what happened and I am in shock and don't have any idea what to say or do." General questions such as "how are you holding up today?" are more helpful. As is "what, if anything, can I do to help?" Rule four, don't avoid me, avoid talking about your children, or be afraid to ask how I am doing now with Ben's death. Rule five, reach out even by email and let the person know you are thinking about them. No need for the perfect follow on to that (see rule one). Be present with those you care about, be gentle, and genuinely ask what they might need. Be supportive and curious and stay connected.

Overall, I have noticed that I grieve differently than most people. I live in the mountains of Colorado and have lived much of my life outdoors. While I like to share outdoor activities with friends, I also, often, prefer to go out alone. The main exception was I would always choose Ben as my most preferred partner from when he was young and I had to slow down for him to when he got older and he had to slow down for me. I feel Ben's presence most when I am out alone in the beauty of nature. At the same time, I felt that for me one of the things that I needed to learn was how to be more open to others, open my heart to those with whom I am connected. I have found it helpful to give myself permission to do less caretaking of others and not agreeing to spend time with others when it does not feel right for me. At the same time, I am looking to connect more deeply in a meaningful way with others when there is that connection of "feeling felt." Overall, find the new balance for you. Life by definition is filled with change and loss.

We have all dealt with loss and will continue to do so. Let's support each other to use difficult events to grow and learn to be our better selves! More tears, more laughter and more love and connectedness; we will get through this together, all in our own way.

Death Is Disruptive

Death is disruptive of all the truths
  that once stabilized my shaky grasp of reality.
In response to your death,
  I can only huddle and wobble and wail,
But maybe, de Chardin is somehow right
  and we are not human beings
  having a spiritual experience,
  but rather spiritual beings,
  having a human experience.
I will still achingly miss you,
  on my earthly journey;
  nothing will change that.
Yet, I am learning to understand
  what being a spiritual being
  might mean for someone like me.
Deep inside my heart,
  a light turns on,
  allowing me an enlarged view
  of the mystery and magic of life.
Awaking in me
  possibilities of living more fully
  because of, or at least in spite of,
  your death.
I travel on hopefully,
  even without your steadying presence
  to guide me on my wobbly way.

December 21, 2019

I Thought We Had Eons

Why me?
Why you?
Who selected who,
     in this topsey-turvy world?
I was your dad.
You were my son.
I am living
     and you are dead.
After years of struggle,
     we beat back the demons
     and reveled in something pure.
Silly me,
     I thought we had eons,
     when only moments
     were ours.

April 22, 2019

Mugged by Reality

The sheer terror of your death
    crept back in last night,
    going around and over the walls
    I had so carefully built
    and assaulted me as I lay awake.
Somehow, it was easier to protect myself
    earlier on when I felt more fully
    the outpouring of love and compassion
    from others and could use it
    as a railing to steady myself.
Now, I have let down my guard,
    lulled into thinking
    the worst is passed,
    and grief did not get the upper hand.
The reality of your absence from my life
    snuck up and mugged me.
Caught me unaware and vulnerable
    in the quiet dark corners of night.

July 10, 2019

Jailed in My Mind

How sad we create our own limited identities,
    against which we fight
    to be more expansive and kind.
We are imprisoned behind walls
    of our own making,
    right here in our own minds.
Small rooms, stark cells,
    with few windows,
    from which we might glimpse,
    the infinite divine.
Our dual role as jailor and inmate
    made easier
    by our failure to see the walls
    or the bigger world left behind.

October 3, 2019

You Are Not Mine

Life is so full of distractions,
    just the thoughts in my head take most of my time.
Then we have roles and restrictions,
    that seem to teach us how to barely connect,
    or connect through silly rules
    that were written for a different time.
You are not mine.

I have the privilege of connecting with you
    if I choose to devote the time.
Our roles make that sometimes possible
    but only when I don't think you are mine.
When I run on a mountain trail,
    I own that place for a time.
When I am more fully present with you,
    I am yours and you are mine.

June 2, 2019

The Only Things Worth Saying

I would love to be able to paint in words
    the magic of the dawning of a new day,
    when darkness plays with light
    and sneaks over the black mountains,
    at first with blue tinges on the margins,
    before the pink and orange highlights
    spring to life.

Better yet, to express somehow
    those feelings inside when I think of you.
The ones that have so many nuances,
    from joyous energy
    to deep longing to hear your voice again
    and to look into your eyes
    experiencing that unstated knowing and connection.

What animates our world
    and makes life worth living
    is intangible.
As elusive as your spirit
    that brought me so much joy
    as well as doubt, fear, confusion, sorrow and love.
The only things worth saying
    are those things that are unsayable.

December 30, 2019

The Why Bother Blues

Some days seem so ordinary at first
    that I forget the pain inside,
    at least for a time or two.
But without you here,
    my world feels empty and gray.
I got the why bother blues.

When you were here
    I thought of you often,
    mostly with joy and love,
    but sometimes with worry,
    sadness, confusion or worse.
After all, you weren't perfect
    nor am I.
I've got the why bother blues.

I longed for the day
    when we had time enough
    to laugh and play and celebrate.
I longed to see you
    full stride in your life,
    happy, successful, and content.
Neither of us did contentment well,
    even as we grew more patient
    with the slow process of change.
Now without you here,
I've got the why bother blues.

I fight off that "so what feeling"
    as I march on alone.

Not being able to check in with you,
      how do I know if where I'm marching
      makes any sense at all.
My world has lost all its color and shine.
You left me with the why bother blues!

December 29, 2019

When Life Slows Down

When life shows down
    and the quiet pries open cracks
    in my fragile construct of reality,
    and all the choices lined up
    in front of me
    seem like useless distractions
    and arbitrary placeholders.
I did many things,
    intently, and mostly well.
Yet now I more often just wonder why.
If life can be so short
    and arbitrary,
    I need to live more fully
    and with intention,
    or just sit around and wonder why.

July 5, 2019

Omens

Some days are harder than others,
when sadness washes over me
    and drags me along
    and buries me in an avalanche of grief.
Hard not to ask then
    where are we/me going
    and does it even matter any more.
Little things make me happy for a while,
    like finding my favorite pen
    lost upside down
    in my pen jar.
Yet, bigger things baffle me,
    like finding a pair of randonee boots
    in a consignment store,
    just like the ones you were wearing
    when you died –
    the only ones there in my size.
Certainly, an omen
    but an omen of what?
What does any of this mean?
I alternate between
    believing in the unseen divine,
    and thinking there is no meaning,
    other than putting one foot in front of the other
    and calling it my path.

October 11, 2019

Happiness

The trouble with happiness
    is not with happiness at all.
The trouble with happiness
    is with the stories we tell.
How I need
    this or that.
How you have
    this or that
    which I want greatly.
By the time I had
    what I thought I needed,
    I'd lost the very thing
    that made me happy
    or would have
    if only I had known.

July 13, 2019

Deciding to Be Happy

I could be happy today
    but have not decided
    yet to do so.
Better to keep my options open
    and not commit.
Hardly my fault
    if nothing exciting happens to me today.
It takes planning
    and early morning action
    to do the things
    that upon reflection
    seem meaningful and worthy
    of my day.
Easier to just do
    that which comes my way.

July 14, 2019

What Matters Enough to Do

If I have money enough
    to live well and travel widely,
    why bother to do the things
    that take more effort
    and require discipline beyond enough.
I don't need to be promoted.
Not sure I want your praise.
My financial planner says I'll be fine
    without further financial success.
I don't think I'll be famous,
    and not sure I'd want to be.
Would be nice to be admired
    or invited on a trip or two.
I'd love to get better
    at skiing powder lines in trees.
I won't turn down
    a chance to coach a leader
    who can make changes in the world.
It mattered more than anything
    to continue to make you proud.
I loved our parallel adventures
    before you left me here alone.
So without a chance to call and talk with you,
    what matters enough to do?

July 14, 2019

Grieving with You

I pretend that I want to see you,
    to offer my feeble hug and empty words.
I need to reach out and comfort you,
    to help me feel like I am doing the right thing.
I'm even surprised that I feel some relief,
    when seeing you is more normal than not.
Yet, truth be told, you scare me in ways
    I cannot even admit to myself.
Your loss and your grief and the terror
    in your eyes when the smile fades,
    threaten my shaky construct of this world.

He wasn't suppose to die,
    not so young, not when he did so much right.
I grieved with you in the early days,
    as any good person would do.
But now I need to build a bigger,
    more complex view of my world,
    or retreat back to my smaller,
    safer fantasy of what should be true.
No one dies too young,
    we all have plenty of time to do
    better tomorrow than today.
Being a good person is just the avoidance
    of doing anything too bad to those we say we love.
The sacred, the divine, our soul purpose,
    are all just words I can safely ignore for now.
Unless that sadness in your eyes,
    scares me into being a better, fuller, more loving me.

April 1, 2019

Endings Can Be So Sad

No, not the ones of loss,
    which, of course, are tragic,
    but rather the ones of gain.
Accomplishing what we set out to do,
    solving the problem,
    gaining the degree,
    mastering the skill.
If the goal was big enough
    and worthy of our effort,
    it came slowly over time.
It humbled us,
    and made us feel unworthy
    and discouraged along the way.
We gave up many times,
    at least in the dark of the night,
    when we settled for a lesser goal,
    one less scary and demanding,
    more easily achieved.
Coming back and going on
    seemed foolish, a silly waste of time,
    like a child's dream of greatness and fame.
Then one day we realize
    we've become that thing we tried to be.
We are a surfer or a skier,
    a doctor or a poet.
No, not great,
    or even recognized,
    just changed somehow within.
Too late, we realize
    that the journey was the prize
    not the end.

December 30, 2019

part two

Making Meaning

People say that what we're all seeking is a meaning for life. I don't think that's what we're really seeking. I think that what we're seeking is an experience of being alive, so that our life experiences on the purely physical plane will have resonances within our own innermost being and reality, so that we actually feel the rapture of being alive.

Joseph Campbell – *The Power of Myth*

Finding Reason for Hope

As a psychologist and an executive coach I have a robust curiosity about what drives our behavior. How do we become who we are? How do we continue to change and grow throughout our lives? Why is it that some people are resilient and overcome adversity and others are run over and struggle to ever get back on track? Why do some people develop and evolve throughout their lives and others seem to stop or even retreat? Why do some people search for and find meaning in their lives, while others are plagued by doubts and a sense of futility?

These questions are not unique to me or new to our times. Aristotle, Plato, Marcus Aurelius, Lucretius and many others throughout history contemplated such questions. Primarily, they were looking for an answer to the major human questions of why am I here and what does it mean to have a life well-lived? What is particularly exciting for us now is we have both the wisdom of the ages passed down to us combined with the availability of new research in neuroscience and related fields. This research has shown us that we are much more capable of change and growth throughout our lifetime than was previously believed. We know that we are all capable of tremendous change in any area where we choose to focus energy and deliberately practice. Our abilities are much less fixed than we thought and growth is much more within reach than we believed. We also see that what we thought made us happy, gave us joy, is not necessarily what did so.

Research on awareness and mindfulness is, at the same time, showing us that we can learn to integrate our brains in more effective ways that can improve our health, slow down aging, and expand our consciousness. We can become that better version of ourselves, who has greater presence with others and more consistent energy to make a difference in the world. We can create the magic that we yearn to experience in our lives. We can learn to be the leaders that our world so desperately needs during these turbulent, unsettling times. We can be our better selves.

Ben lived his life fully even with the ups and downs he experienced. He embodied the spirit of continuous learning, pushing his limits, and bringing a joyous presence into the lives he touched. At the same time, he struggled to make sense and find balance. I loved our conversations about these concepts as well as the joy we had playing outside – "dancing on the edge."

In whatever time I have left here, I hope to continue to learn and change and grow as I did in relation to Ben. I have more questions than answers and know deep inside that I am here because I still have work (and play) to do. I have faith in a larger purpose even if I don't always know what that means. Overall, I see believing in something more as a win-win proposition; either there is "something more" and I'm working towards it, or there is nothing more after death and I lived my life to its fullest and enjoyed the ride (and continued to make Ben proud). I do believe that there is something more and, somehow, it is connected to love, compassion, and connection more than money, power, and judgment. And, just a reminder, they call it faith because the big questions are unanswerable. I hope you choose to believe; in life, in yourself, in making the world a better place! I hope that you work towards finding meaning in your life and in the process help create the world you want to live in and leave to your children and grandchildren.

Making Meaning

Sitting on the floor by the heat of my fire,
    looking up at the tall, crammed bookshelves
    filled with books in all shapes and sizes and colors.
Books filled with words, ideas, and struggles.
Written by real people
    to communicate stories and concepts.
How did these particular books
    find their way into my life?
What have I learned by living with them,
    sometimes reading them,
    sometimes thinking about them,
    sometimes trying to tell others about them,
    sometimes writing about the stories they told me?
They call out to me
    to tell my own stories
    about what I know and don't know.
Words transformed into meaning
    in a strange alchemical sort of way.
Bits of energy created within the neurons
    of my mind.
No, not created,
    only discovered,
    when the flow of awareness
    interacts with memories and sensations,
    and particles of thoughts
    are combined with heat and hurt,
    within the burning desire to make sense.
Trying to make sense
    about what it means to be alive
    and where we were before being born

and went after we died.
Making some meaning
    to guide me on my way.

January 13, 2020

Are You Breathing Just a Little?

Mary Oliver asks us,
    "Listen, are you breathing just a little
    and calling it a life?"
The phrase brings a smile
    followed by questions.
Am I? Are we?
How do I/we know?
How do we even begin to comprehend the question,
    not to mention, truly know the answer?
The easy answer
    is, of course, yes.
After all, my life is bounded
    by my first breath
    and my last.
What I call my life is merely
    what happens during all those breaths in between.
Besides, I am just visiting this world for a time,
    and I came without a decent map.
(Or maybe I had one and
    lost it on the way.)
The sages agree that we all have a larger soul purpose
    even though they fall short on helping us know
    what that reason might be.
To be alive and awake more fully
    means following your spirit
    and trying to make a difference
    with people and places
    that mean the most to you.
Be creative, silly, and kind.
Do hard things with a purpose

that you can't do at first,
and fall in love with the process
more than the results.
So ask yourself more often,
are you breathing just a little,
and calling it a life?

July 6, 2019

Finding Our Way

Wayfinding research tells us that humans
    are not particularly good at finding our way
    in the world without sight and landmarks to guide us.
Blindfolded, we tend to walk in circles
    of 66 feet in diameter
    when unable to see the horizon
    and without any worthwhile goal in mind.
Yet, goals seem arbitrary
    once we get above the basics to survive.
If Maslow was right,
    self actualization is a lofty abstraction
    hovering somewhere above all other needs,
    rather than a burning desire
    like water, food, and sex.
No wonder we spend so much of our lives
    going around in circles,
    repeating our mistakes
    just trying to get by.
Free will means we get to choose
    to live intentionally or not.
We are free to just spiral around
    or to find our way
    somewhere meaningful
    connecting to others
    with hearts and eyes
    wide open.

January 31, 2020

Travel with Me

Home to the green of spring,
contrasted with the winter white up high.
Home to sitting quietly by the fire with coffee,
contrasted with the whirl of travel and work.
When you were here on this earth,
that all seemed more than enough.
Now that you have left this earthly life,
I sense a need for something more.
Why am I here when you are gone?
Why did you come into my life?
and then leave so soon?
I don't reflect enough
on where we come from before life,
when reflecting on where you went after yours.
I'm ill-prepared for either conversation,
and have met few who seem to do better or know more.
I could use a wise friend or two,
not necessarily with answers, just appreciating the
questions would do,
(though answers would be welcome too).
Yes, I need someone like you,
who journeyed with me and shared my path,
appreciated both the struggle and sporadic joy.
Knowing there was more to do,
when facing the uncertainty of what and why.

June 1, 2019

Mountain Paths

I have guided earthly paths,
    helping others to heights unknown.
After experiencing mountain beauty,
    the flatlands rarely move me.
My spirit, like yours, was set free
    in the rarified air without trees.
If God is beauty, we were blessed,
    to have served at the altar of the divine.
Now I have a challenge, more daunting yet,
    to know your spirit without you here.
Come and guide me on the paths
    to places, for me, unknown.
Help me quiet my mind and strengthen my will,
    so I can experience heaven and you.

June 6, 2019

Me in Relationship to You

Me in relationship to you
    I like the texture of that phrase.
Certainly more than the possessive nouns
    like father, son, husband, or brother,
    which come loaded with meaning.
    obligation, rights, and claims.
 Scripts to live up to, or run from,
    even if we did not agree
    to the contract they implied.

Me in relationship to you
    empowers me and you.
Asks us to define the form and clarify our intent
    to energize the ebb and flow
    of our connection across space and time.

Philosophers and sages wiser than me
    debate how we came into our lives.
Was there choice involved
    and sacred contracts fairly made?
Karma to be worked through
    in the play between me and you?

An intriguing concept
    even if unknown and unknowable.
Did we agree to play roles,
    that connect us on this earthly sphere,
    where the relationship
    has more meaning than the role?

Me in relationship to you,
     is how I choose to remember us.
I am proud of how we traveled together
     and love to hold you in my heart.

June 9, 2019

Dancing on the Edge

Ben, you were my magic being
        sent here for me to shelter
        and care for in ways
        that opened my heart.
You grew into a man
        who touched others deeply
        through wit and wisdom
        as you played on the edge.
You were my soul mate,
        who agreed to come with me
        to play out our karma
        in a dance I barely understood.
Now you are gone,
        at least in bodily form,
        and I try to dance on the edge alone
        in ways that would make you proud.

October 13, 2019

Faith

I am free to believe or not,
    in any story that helps or hurts.
They call it faith,
    because the big questions are unanswerable.
No one gets out alive.
No one comes back to tell.
If I had to guess,
    the answer contains
    love, compassion, and connection,
    more than money, power, and judgment.
I love the vast array of stories
    we humans have created
    every culture their creation myth,
    every religion their steadfast beliefs.
Although I struggle with the damage
    we sometimes inflict on others
    who don't believe as we do.
We need to ask ourselves,
    does our tribe's story and beliefs
    create more joy and love in our lives,
    more sharing and connection with others,
    more peace and compassion in the world?
Is our story strong enough to stand up and help,
    when death comes knocking on our door?
The story I tell myself
    is that I have faith in a spiritual world
    where the struggle to be my better self has meaning
    beyond this moment of this day.
In reality, some days, I do,
    and some days, I don't,

have faith in much of anything.
But, I ask myself,
    even if my story is not right or fully true,
    does it help me bring
    more joy, love, and hope into the world?
If so, I have faith for now
    that my story is the best I can do
    as I try to make meaning
    out of the loss of you.

January 3, 2020

The Path to the Unknown

What I know so clearly
    gets in the way of the unknown.
When you were here
    it felt safe and fun
    to explore in conversation
    what we only glimpsed and did not know.

Now that you are gone
    what is here and knowable
    feels flat and incomplete.
I want, I need, I am drawn
    towards something greater,
    something less knowable
    with my conscious mind.
The spiritual world is more compelling
    since you are there
    and I am here.

June 25, 2019

Believing Is Seeing

I want to experience your presence
  in my earthly life.
I am longing to sense you
  and the magic of the spiritual world.
I tell myself
  I believe.
I even have begun to look closer
  at the margins of experience
  with open eyes
  and a sense of possibility.
Yet, I am like a blind man
  who is open to seeing Mount Sopris
  while lacking the capacity to do so
  in the darkness of his world.
Even though he believes
  it would be wondrous
  to see that majestic mountain
  covered with summer snow.
Luckily for me, I was taught to see
  or maybe just developed sight
  since everyone assumed I would.
Now I long to see the spiritual
  just as mystics somehow do.
I can continue to be the blind man,
  disbelieving the heavenly vision is true.
Or I can learn to see with my heart
  what I know is here and contains you.

May 18, 2019

My Five Sense Logic

What I know to be true
    keeps me from knowing what is true.
What my senses sense
    keep me separated from you.
How do I transcend
    my five sense logic?
How do I add
    something new?
It is easy to say
    choose love over fear.
It is harder to know
    what that really means,
    today, right now,
    in this moment of my life.
How do I learn
    to sense what I now
    only hope is true?
How do I learn
    to sense the beauty
    that is you?

July 4, 2019

Beyond My Senses

What does it mean to be alive and awake?
What should I do?
How should I be?
Who will I become?
All great questions to orient my life,
  to define myself beyond what I know and do.
My senses tell me
  what is real.
At least as much as they know how.
Life seems so beautifully mysterious
  precisely because of what
  my senses, by definition, cannot touch or see.
How ironic we use the phrase
  I cannot make sense of that.
Such a wise statement
  even when I fail to notice the wisdom.
The harder I struggle to know,
  the less I trust in the infinite beauty
  of the world beyond my senses.
Then, in random moments,
  I'm able to let go
  and float silently into the vast unknown.

July 20, 2019

Snowy Morning

The sage glows crystalline white in the early morning sun,
    allowing my awareness to rest in the cold peace
    of frosty coverings of all I sense
    underneath and within.
Inside, my fire burns with orange-blue flames
    that dance to their own tune.
Life giving melodic movement
    animating the still air.
What can I learn from the absolute stillness
    of the sage holding its breath,
    lest it disturb the snow crystals
    stacked so lightly everywhere?
What can I learn from the animating warmth of the fire,
    giving freely of its energy,
    blessing me with rich abundance?
I feel neither still nor abundant.
Yet, I am both when I open to my breath,
    and rest in awareness of all that is.

January 23, 2020

Early Morning

I love watching night
    turn into day.
The texture of light
    in the high mountain snow.
Colors emerging
    then fading into brightness.
Too early to call someone
    I don't know well.
This was my time to connect
    with my mom when she was here.
This was the time to connect with you
    after she was gone.
This was the time to remind myself
    I belonged somewhere
    and was connected to someone I loved.
I sit alone in this early morning light,
    glad for my solitude
    and freedom from obligations.
I imagine my rich community
    of family and friends,
    who know me and care.
Without you to talk to
    where do I belong?

June 15, 2019

Lost in the Wilderness

The human tendency is to speed up
    when we are lost.
This has always been most obvious to me
    when I am lost in wilderness,
    with fewer distractions and no one else to blame.
Since you died,
    I am often lost
    in the wilderness of my grief,
    moving faster or not at all.
Just when I most need
    to be still and move slowly,
    deliberately sensing my world more fully,
    I am agitated and scared,
    afraid to slow down.
My survival training taught me to make stories
    and remember them when lost in the woods
    to help me slow down and stay present.
Sometimes, stories help me now as well,
    in spite of their power to scare me more,
    and make me spin even faster than before.
But really the problem is not the speed,
    rather the lack of presence it creates,
    further disconnecting me from you
    and the comforting web of our lives.

August 4, 2019

Climbing Sopris

Walk with me in this quiet valley
    of unspoiled green hills.
Walk with me on high mountain ridges,
    calling our names.
I am blessed
    to look out on the snowcapped peak of Sopris
    with dreams of climbing up
    her naked ridges still.
Will you be there
    when I head up in the cold dark time
    before the light of the sun?
Will you be waiting for me
    in the shelter of the summit,
    enjoying the warmth of sunlight
    served with the awe of distant views?
We had in common
    a love of powerful natural places,
    where the price of admission
    was measured not by what you had,
    but by what you we were willing to give.
Walk with me once more
    to this magical place up high.
Help me understand
    why I am here and you are gone.
Teach me how to live without you
    and a reason why.

August 27, 2019

Climbing Alone

I am driving in the dark to climb Sopris alone,
    feeling shaky and uncertain
    about my lack of preparation, my fitness, my resolve.
The day starts well as darkness fades to light
    and movement, any movement up,
    reminds me of who I am and what I know.
I work hard at being present
    with my breath, not lost in my head,
    considering the vibration of me in this space.
Sopris is not technical, in a climbing sense,
    just long and steep,
    with false summits and rocky loose footing.
Here I am in this vast solitude,
    all alone in the thin air up high,
    blessed to experience this sublime altar.
Later, I can romanticize the stark beauty of the climb;
    now, I notice my slow pace and the difficulty
    of little things like eating, drinking, and taking off a layer.
Close up the route seems confusing
    even to just follow the ridgeline
    to the first of the twin summits.
Before and after, this is just a story;
    now, it is a tumble of thoughts and feelings
    as I go on to the second summit unsure.
Time on the summit is more a blur
    than I imagined in my pre-climb thoughts,
    less about sensing you than taking care of me.
I am not lost; I am heading down Sopris,
    yet, there is no promise that my tired legs
    and wobbly attention will hold.

Time melts away in spite of my haste.
    I work to stay present and notice
    my pains, my breathing, my sense of unfair suffering.
I tell myself, let's not make a walk up a mountain
    into something more heroic and daring
    or into something less magical and divine.

September 28, 2019

Sacred Mountain

The Utes believed as do I
    that Sopris is a sacred mountain.
How could she not be,
    just look up at her majestic form.
I assume a female presence,
    a Mother Goddess, like Everest in Nepal.
Beautiful and shining out,
    waiting to be underestimated,
    glad to be radiant and welcoming,
    powerful and inspiring.
Encouraging me and other pilgrims
    to get over ourselves,
    quit the doubts and fears,
    and celebrate the journey up.
All pilgrimages are ultimately
    journeys within.
All journeys are ultimately
    journeys home.

October 6, 2019

Maybe Death Is Like Birth

Being born must have seemed like death,
    a terrifying change to all
    I had ever known.
Expelled from my comfortable existence
    in a warm safe place
    where all I had to do
    was float and be.
So what that my life in the womb had its limitations,
    where I was confined
    with limited consciousness or choice.
My life in there was all I had ever known.
I did not willingly choose
    to get expelled from my safe knowing
    into the cold, thin air of life.
Everyone around me celebrated
    the joyous occasion of my birth,
    with the endless possibilities
    of who I could now become.
I cried for what I lost,
    the warm comfort of my known.
So maybe dying is like birth,
    an expulsion from the safe known
    into the once invisible divine.
The return to a warm, magical place
    where I can do no wrong
    and the white light of love envelops me.

August 18, 2019

Only Now

Life is made up of transitions,
    just look at seasons,
    children growing and developing,
    day turning to night and back again.
Yet, we think of transitions,
    when we think of them at all,
    as the exception,
    not the rule.
We expect predictability
    and we get flow.
We know from early on
    there is a cycle of life.
In childhood we are told
    all living beings die.
Yet, we are constantly surprised
    by change.
Death is an affront
    to our cozy narrative
    of a predictable journey
    with knowable landmarks;
    and even guard rails,
    if we need them.
Yes, we will die one day,
    since everyone does.
But it's odd to talk about it out loud;
    worse yet to explore and embrace
    the mystery of that unknown.
We comfortably live as if we're immortal,
    forgetting to revel in the magic of moments,
    and the incomprehensibleness of being alive.

To live more fully takes courage,
    when there is no promise
    of tomorrow
    or even later today;
    only now.

October 29, 2019

I Am Home

I am home,
    even if still figuring out
    what that really means.
Back from traveling,
    while not quite back
    into my routines of being.
Catching up.
Settling in.
Washing off the traces of travel
    and enjoying the warm comfort of home.
I am busy making up stories
    in answer to questions
    of where was I?
    and how did it go?
Stories that smooth over
    the rough edges
    when I momentarily forget
    who I have been
    and how I even know.
Traveling makes it possible
    to discover something new
    outside my simple, known world
    and the stories I tell
    of who I am,
    when I am just being me.
I am home,
    yet not quite settled into
    the limits of who I was
    before I left.

November 11, 2019

The Toast I Did Not Give

I'm honored to be here
    to celebrate with you.
To hear the toasts of joy,
    give voice to the magic of wedding moments,
    commemorate lives yet lived and
    imagine the possibilities of dreams coming true.

I don't know you well
    and many not at all.
Yet, even though a stranger,
    I'm here to toast the bride and groom.
To help them, and all the rest,
    to envision their long and happy marriage.
I wish you all the best.

Like all of you,
    I want my message
    to be bright and cheery,
    hopeful, witty, and, possibly, wise.
Yet, I must share a secret
    about lives well-lived,
    and marriages built to last.

The secret is not secret,
    but, easily forgotten and ignored until too late.
Rather than envisioning a long and happy life
    that rolls on with time enough tomorrow
    for all your earthly dreams
    focus instead on being fully present,
    each moment of each day.
There is no true promise of future time
    beyond this moment now.

Life can be unexpectantly short,
    with no guarantee of imagined tomorrows.
So live and love as if today
    is all you have.
And tomorrow is an imagined gift,
    that may or may not ever be opened.

June 18, 2019

The Anniversary

Today is the anniversary of your death
    the calendar tells me.
But I'm confused,
        isn't every day an anniversary
        just measured in different, arbitrary ways
        of counting and keeping track?
I understand that some like round numbers
        and we all prefer the system our tribe agreed to use.
So, it has been 365 sunsets since you died.
Yet, it hurt as much or more at 39 and 267 as it does today.
Still, I have other ways of keeping track,
        like how many breaths have I taken since you left.
How many times have I written in my journal
        and wanted to talk to you about it and couldn't?
How many times did I forget momentarily
        that you are not here
        and was stabbed in the heart once again?
Now, I need to ask how many more breaths or sunsets
        will there be before my death?
What else shall I do as I sit missing you?
Do I move faster and do more
        to create meaning in my life?
Or wait patiently for the silent approach of death,
        focusing on what I lost
        rather than what I have to gain?
If I had known that today was going to be the anniversary
        of your death two years before,
        how would I have used the breaths or the sunsets
        we had left, differently, more intentionally?
Would we have connected more powerfully,

lived more joyously,
laughed more generously,
or engaged more deeply
during our last perfect day together?
How shall we celebrate today
living fully and soulfully
whatever days we have left together?
Why is it easier to mourn than celebrate?

January 25, 2020

part three

Finding Our Way

And the day came when the risk to remain tight in a bud was more painful than the risk it took to blossom.

Anaïs Nin – *Diaries Vol 1, 1931 – 1934*

What We Have, Who We Are, What We Can Become

Neuroscientists point out that we are not wired for happiness and joy. While some people, in Jonathan Haidt's words, "won the cortical lottery," meaning that their set range for happiness is higher than others who are more anxious and scared; mostly, we are all more prone to doubt and fear than optimism and positivity. Added to this, the speed of change, the flow of information, and the overcrowding and degradation of our natural spaces have all increased, while our sense of community, connection and trust in our institutions has been seriously eroded. Not surprisingly, these factors and others have resulted in greater depression, hopelessness, and anger for most people. Even people, who seem to have enviable lives with more resources than most, are found on closer study to generally feel like imposters and frauds. The millionaires envy the billionaires while the research on happiness shows that beyond a basic amount to get by, more money does not increase our happiness and sense of well-being.

I have found in my lifelong work in psychology and leadership coaching that most people dream of a more meaningful life in which they can feel they are making a positive difference in the world or at least in some small part of the world where they live and work. They just do not have a model of what that would look like, where to start, and what they might need to change. The model that most people have grown up with is that they need to fix what is wrong, eliminate their bad habits, and be somehow more perfect or more worthy. Even the field of psychology, which is ostensibly about helping people become emotionally healthy, in reality, has mostly focused on labeling what is wrong and attempting to fix problem areas. Years ago, psychologists such as myself went through graduate school and were awarded a doctorate in psychology without ever being required to take a course that focused on the definition of a healthy, happy person, let alone on the best ways to attain that elusive goal.

In the late 1990's a group of psychologists led by Martin Seligman came together to create and encourage a research focus on "Positive Psychology." Rather than focus on pathology and problems, they began a quest to define what a happy, well- adjusted human looked like and the knowable, doable steps that created more of that sense of happiness and well being in people's lives. Broadly speaking, they worked to define health as not just the elimination of problems and disease but the presence of positive, sustainable ways of being in the world that lead to satisfaction, contentment and, yes, even happiness.

In the last 20 years, more and more has been learned about happiness, positivity, and what helps create in people a sense of well-being and purpose in their lives. We have come to know that individuals are capable of continuing to grow and change over their lifetimes and that, when they do continue to evolve as people, they follow known developmental pathways. At the same time, research shows us that most adults stop developing and growing sometime in their mid to late twenties. If they do start to grow and develop again later, it is most often after 40 to 50 and they only do so if they consciously make an effort to understand who they are and who they want to become. Such growth through more evolved stages of adult development, when it happens, follows specific paths and, overall, moves the person into a more complex pattern of thought, and a greater sense of connection with others. There are known stages of adult development including spiritual development and leadership development similar to a child growing from magical thinking to concrete operations to abstract thinking.

Just to be clear, I am not "more wired for joy" than others. I am not a starry eyed poet caught in the world of unicorns and rainbows. I came from an engineering and science background where you are not paid to be optimistic. Ben's death is and will remain a huge challenge in my life. Some days feel bleak and gray even in the bright sunshine of our western mountains. What I have learned so far is that while I need to allow myself whatever sad and dark feelings come up for me, I, at the same time, need to work on learning to control my mind and open my heart to positive energy, goodness, and love. The better I get at creating my own positive presence, the more I have to offer the world and the people I have the privilege to work with as a psychologist and a leadership coach.

Ben's death has created a sense of urgency for me. Today when I was meditating with five minutes left in one of the guided meditations I use, the thought entered my mind "what if I only had five minutes to prepare for my impending death?" What would I do with so little time and the scary sense of urgency it would create, besides struggling with grasping and letting go? What would I do if I had longer, 15 minutes, six months, or 20 years? In reality, I don't know how to prepare other than doing what I am doing now, trying to live with more intention and paying more attention to how I am spending my time.

Shouldn't that be one of the main goals in all of our lives, to prepare for the death we know will come? After all, we can agree that "no one gets out alive." Just because you and I don't know if we have five minutes or 20 years or more makes no difference. Questions about who we are, why we are here, and what do we need to accomplish in whatever time we have left seem critically important. Certainly they have been for me as I learn to live with Ben's death.

I remember reading several years ago the book *Chasing Daylight: How My Forthcoming Death Transformed My Life* by Eugene O'Kelly. In it, the CEO of KPMG writes about finding out that he had less than six months to live due to a recently discovered inoperable brain tumor. What would sound like a depressing title turned out to be an inspirational memoir reflecting on living a balanced and meaningful life. Mr. O'Kelly talked about being so lucky that he actually knew how long he had to live and could more consciously prepare to leave this world. He described how he approached each day and each person in his life, trying to have the perfect moments and days with them and not wasting time on less essential conversations or connecting with those who were not the most important people in his life.

Buddhism talks about the aim of life is finding your purpose and living it fully. Life and death are but two phases of a continuum. We are energy flowing through our life and our death (and, in the Buddhist belief, flowing on into our next lives). I am not wise enough or enlightened enough to have reached that realization. Nor have I met many who have seemed to figure all this out. The one notable exception for me was the time I was able to be in the presence of the Dalai Lama.

I do believe that awareness of death enables us to treasure our lives and awakens us to the preciousness of whatever time we have here before we die. I also believe that Ben lived well due to understanding this truth, at some level. Those of us who were lucky enough to share time with him benefitted from his energy, enthusiasm, determination, and sheer will to live meaningfully and completely. We can all live more purposeful and fulfilling lives if we learn to treat life as a precious gift and our journey as one of discovery. We can learn to pay attention to and celebrate the positive energy we create along the way both for ourselves and those whose lives we touch.

Fall Equinox

The equinox of Fall is upon us,
    marking the sun passing over the equator
    on its way south for winter.
Grasses turn yellow
    with leaves not far behind.
 Late blooming flowers
    still feed the hummingbirds
    for a short time more.
The snow on Sopris,
    which has lasted the year,
    now waits in welcome
    for reinforcements soon to come.
The warm vibrancy of summer
    fades into the colder stillness
    of peaceful times alone.
The Buddha pushes us
    to recognize that dying
    is not an event
    but rather a process
    going on all the time.
A succession of extremely short-
    lived moments like the seasons
    recreating themselves
    as Autumn comes on strong.
Enlightenment is accepting
    our place in this process
    without grasping
    or giving up.

September 22, 2019

Dawn

The morning light
    hits the top of Sopris
    a little later each day.
As I reset my internal clock
    and celebrate
    being up early enough
    to watch the dark
    fade into light.
I experience
    the pinks blooming
    and fading,
    teaching me to fully enjoy the show.
Not grasping too tightly
    that which I like more
    and pushing away
    that which I like less.
The movement of the light show
    is its meaning,
    just as in my life,
    not the scenes and moments
    I like more or less.

August 29, 2019

Life Is a Pageant

We are all more
    powerful than we allow
    ourselves to know.
Scared by our power,
    we play lesser roles
    so as not to upset others
    who need to see us
    as less than
    rather than in our full light.
Or so we tell ourselves.
When in reality it is we
    who are afraid
    to shine out
    into the world with all the power
    of who we really are.
So ask yourself,
    who would you be
    if you lived knowing
    you are more?
What light are you
    withholding from the world?
Life is a pageant
    in which we play roles
    that distract us
    from knowing
    who we really are
    and why we are here.

May 19, 2020

Here I Am

Here I am
    in a world of my choosing,
    a landscape of my making.
Quietly absorbed
    in the magic beauty of sunrise on Sopris.
Here I am
    centered and contained,
    potential energy,
    rather than kinetic movement.
 Whispering to myself words,
    so fragile and strong.
Registering images,
    transitory and etched in time.
I am strong and powerful.
Solid in my being.
Feeling able
    to influence broadly and quietly,
    yet, not needing to at all.
I am reminded of your growing power
    and quiet strength, last time
    we shared space and time.
The sparkle showed in your pride
    in rehabbing your leg,
    the big mountains you planned to ski,
    the hedge fund you founded,
    and the people you touched.
We were stronger together,
    each doubled by the dreams
    of the other.
Now your powerful presence fills me

with both sadness and promise,
when sensed
in early morning light.

August 5, 2019

The Improbability of Our Lives

Do you know how improbable it is
    that you and I are here?
How unusual that this blue planet
    even supports life?
How amazing that our DNA
    somehow came together just so?
Maybe, if we could more fully grasp
    the magnitude of the miracle of life in general,
    and our lives in particular,
    we would live our lives more fully
    with the reverence they deserve.
After all, there are no ordinary moments,
    no time to kill without wounding eternity.
Who are you?
Who am I?
What will take our breath away?
What difference will these lives of ours make?
When working with high performance teams
    I ask, did your presence here today
    make a difference in any meaningful way?
We need to also ask,
    do the lives we are living
    make a meaningful difference
    to someone or something in ways that matter?
Why squander our "precious human lives?"
Why mourn when we are gone
    that which we failed to celebrate
    when it was here.
Living more magically and fully
    with love and laughter

counts for more
than rivers of tears at our funerals.

March 13, 2020

A Lion Morning

This feels like a lion morning,
    one where I will glimpse
    a lion moving
    through sage
    at sunrise.
Momentarily seeing
    that majestic creature looking
    so improbably long
    with her four foot tail.
Confirming the beauty my rushing heart
    so desperately wants to see.

This feels like a lion morning
    even if I have only rarely glimpsed
    a lion moving through the sage
    while looking out
    into the beauty of nature
    at sunrise.
My life is richer
    knowing that such creatures
    exist around me still.
My life is fuller
    knowing that I can look out my window
    into the beauty of nature
    at sunrise.

September 1, 2019

The Flow of Life

I am more like the evergreen
    holding tightly to my needles
    than the aspen with her flamboyant
    show of color foretelling
    her shameless disrobing
    for all the world to see.
I want to shout out
    "Have you no pride!"

Yet I know my prudish sensitivity
    only hides my envy of her embrace
    of the flow of life we all desire.
I will get there eventually
    one needle at a time.
Reluctantly, painfully holding on too long
    to what needs to be shed
    so that the new growth can emerge.

I know I am not this body
    but, my, it seems like home.
I know that dying is the key
    to living more fully.
Dying in small ways
    makes way for the rebirth to come.

October 18, 2020

Karmic Choice

Life can be more intentional
    than the randomness our world implies.
We are set in motion,
    in a world of choice and purpose,
    even when we have forgotten
    who we are and from whence we came.
We journey through our life,
    behaving in ordinary ways,
    doing the expected and pre-ordained.
 Yet, at our best, we go beyond,
    stretching ourselves to be more,
    in spite of the scary unknown.
We entertain ourselves with stories,
    that may or may not be true,
    in which we play victim or hero,
    and sometimes both.
Yet, freewill is more than choosing
    to do what seems needed
    in the shadowbox of our imagined life.
Karmic choice plays a subtle tune,
    to which we dance,
    moving between who we think we are
    and our larger self
    waiting to be rediscovered.

September 15, 2019

Belief

I, like you,
   started out believing
   in a more limited story of me,
   given by others
   and reinforced by my lack of dreams.

And, like you,
   I can choose to believe
   in a bigger me
   grown from the seeds
   of hope and reflected experience.

I now know
   that living large
   begins with awareness
   and the ability to be present
   in spite of the noise of the world,
   combined with monkeys
   running wild in my mind.

You and I
   need to ask ourselves
   what matters enough
   that we will go out and do it
   even when the pain is real
   and fear seems stronger than love.

We know deep down
   that failure is the inability to let ourselves try
   and success means embracing the fact

that we are all super humans
waiting to know our purpose
and master our craft.

June 25, 2019

Chanting in the Kiva

It's all about connection,
    they said, as we sat
    in their beautiful kiva to chant.
Bring your own intentions
    and open yourself.
Or better yet,
    allow yourself to be open.
Pay attention to the vibrations,
    absorb the energy.
I'd like to say I had magical revelations,
    was enlightened in some secret way.
I can say I was open and impressed
    at what was created and shared.

In my dream the next morning,
    I remember wondering
    if I possessed something they needed,
    and needed something they had.
My inner voice corrected me,
    see if you have something they want to learn,
    and if they have something to teach you.

September 23, 2019

Entropy

When not moving towards integration
 complex systems, like our lives,
 either move towards chaos or rigidity.
To avoid that, we need to learn how to better regulate
 the flow of energy and information in our minds.
We are emergent, changing beings
 who will be different ten years from now
 in ways not knowable today,
 regardless of what we do or don't do.
So ask yourself more often
 are you moving towards worthwhile goals?
Are you learning to love and connect more fully
 with people and concepts that create
 the vision of who you hope to be?
Or are you shrinking and playing it safe
 making excuses for your reduced presence
 and fear of the unknown?
Are you manufacturing lives that are doable,
 safe and familiar
 with just enough novelty
 to stay semi-conscious?
Are your choices limited by your abilities and resources,
 or your lack of imagination?
What is your vision
 of who you will be in three years?
Does it take your breath away?

February 5, 2020

Rays of Hope

Sun shining through gray-black clouds,
    lighting up the improbably green,
    snow-frosted grass and sage.
Who am I not to rejoice
    with awe and gratitude,
    even after the landscape is shaded
    by fast moving clouds
    who have their own schedules to keep?
My world is smaller
    without you in it with me.
Or possibly so much larger
    since I am drawn out of myself
    into the mysterious expanse
    of the cosmic universe all around me.
Searching for your comforting presence,
    I stumble across my own.

April 12, 2020

Reflections on a Peaceful Morning

I hope to see a mountain lion
    in the predawn light
    of this peaceful morning.
I am willing to be patient and quiet,
    and worthy.
I am appreciative of the rosy light
    up high on Sopris
    as I scan for movement in the grass and sage.
I take time to reflect in my journal
    on my memories of you and I.
I am grateful for the time
    we shared last year around this date.
Then, suddenly I am aware
    of how my silly desire to see a lion
    has made the perfect beauty
    of this scene seem flat
    and plain and empty, just like
    the miraculous world of my life
    without you in it.
A humming bird eats from a flower close by
    as sunlight illuminates the grass and sage.
    So begins another day.

September 25, 2019

Observations

Have you ever been aware
    of being aware?
Being mindful of mindfulness itself?
Not focused on the object of awareness,
    but rather the process of being aware?
Floating in awareness.
Resting in awareness,
    effortlessly, open, mindful, and aware.
Connected to everything and nothing
    since there is no me to connect,
    or judge,
    or think,
    or not connect.
Visualize the plane of awareness
    from which consciousness arises,
    where everything is possible
    before we create our reality
    from our thoughts and beliefs.
Physicists tell us energy is potential
    before it becomes manifest.
Practice choosing to be alive and aware
    in this moment, now.
Practice being aware of awareness.

January 12, 2020

Luminosity

I am a luminescent being.
If I am not this body or this mind,
    then what or who am I?
All that I am is the magical white light of love,
    part of universal consciousness,
    the essence of spirit and awareness,
    energetic formlessness, sheltered
    in a perfect human body.
While in this body
    I need to manifest my essence
    through my physical being
    and my mental capacity.
Hard not to get confused
    about who I am and am not,
    and what I am here to do.
Kornfield advises us
    not to forget our zip code,
    as we seek our essential being.
Somehow, I need to combine
    doing and being, even if I don't yet know how.
Living in the positive energy of gratitude and love
    manifesting through universal consciousness.
I am me and not me,
    the white light of love
    working through and transcending
    my egoic self,
    whatever that means.

October 2, 2019

Meditation

Why meditate,
    if as the sages say,
    I am perfect as I am?
If all I have is now,
    where do I look for joy?
I take one more breath,
    to bring me back to now.
I ask what is here now?
Then I ask, what else is here now?
Trying not to be resigned to all that I cannot control.
Centered inside myself,
    watching my breath emerge.
Sitting quietly when I can.
Getting blown around by cosmic winds
    and coming back to what is.
At the same time, I create
    what comes next,
    as much as witnessing
    what happens in the swirling process of life.
How do I reconcile Doing and Being?
How do I create joy
    without getting snagged by grasping?
I am learning to be centered
    in the "nowness" of this moment.
Learning to be centered,
    in the newness of this moment.
Learning to be who I am.

December 27, 2019

Powder Turns

The photograph on my wall
    captures the magic
    of powder turns through trees
    on a crystal clear, sunlit morning.
Just as I remember that day,
    that perfect moment of time.
Yet, it is both inspirationally true
    and a grand illusion.
After all,
    I like remembering my perfect turns
    more than the uncertainty
    with which I made them.
The tumble of thoughts in my head
    I needed to breathe away
    as I rested my weary legs.
I can now safely forget
    that they even existed
    in that clear morning air.
My life, unlike the photo,
    is perfect because of my fragility,
    not in spite of it.
My life has meaning
    because of my heroic journey
    into the confusion
    of my day.

August 28, 2019

What If?

What if I truly knew in my deepest part of being
    that these moments
    that make up today
    were sparks of divine energy
    given to me as a gift?
Would I treat them
    the same?
Would I scatter them
    haphazardly?
Would I forget to notice
    the vibrancy and possibility they bring?
This gift of time
    I throw into some dark corner
    with other discarded bits
    that did not come wrapped up
    in bright paper and shrill ribbons.
What if I could treat this moment
    as the sacred gift it is?
What if I used it to create
    that which we all need
    to shine as we celebrate
    the magic of our lives?

October 7, 2019

Attunement

I am the breather
    and the breath.
I am the subject
    and the object of my thoughts.
My awareness
    arises and fades away.
I watch my thoughts
    without being them.
I watch you,
    breathing and thinking.
I move from not being you,
    to knowing and feeling you.
My heart opens.
We are part of the same whole.

August 11, 2019

Life Force

What is that unknowable force,
    that unspoken energy,
    which animates our being
    and directs our awareness
    to the process of being alive?
We are all magical beings
    who come into our lives
    full of potential
    and only partially formed.
We are molded and shaped
    by forces and family,
    parents and circumstances,
    choices made
    as well as paths not taken.
Never too late
    to recreate our story.
Be something more.
Touch others and celebrate with
    new dance steps
    we had been too fearful to try
    until we realized
    we had nothing to lose.
We are loved
    and cherished dearly.
A piece of that unknowable force
    that animates our being
    with the magic
    of our creative potential
    to flourish and thrive.

May 14, 2020

I Am Here and Still You Are Gone

Dear Ben, as summer begins to feel cooler
    around the edges,
as Sopris calls out to me
    to come visit up high,
as fires burn the canyons around me
    turning our world smoky and scary,
as Covid still reigns supreme
    creating more hurt and pain and fear,
a year and a half without you has passed—
    still I am here and you are gone.

I thought I would somehow just dry up and dissolve into dust,
    blow away and leave no trace.
When I did not,
    I put on my socks and a brave face,
and ventured into a ravaged landscape
    to find purpose and meaning,
    still wondering why I am here and you are gone.

In other hard times, I was sustained by an inner thought
    that the universe wanted me to succeed.
Instinctively, now I have come to the choice
    we all have to make in the face of unspeakable tragedy.
Either the world is random and risky and meaningless,
    or things happen for a reason
    and life is a journey towards acceptance and love
    and a semblance of meaning.

So here I am writing poetry of all things,
    hoping to make a difference somehow

in this world of ours on the brink of destruction.
Where fear and greed and anger and distrust
        seem to be winning over hope, joy, and compassion.
Having faith means there is a chance that I am wrong
        about meaning and healing and rebirth.

As we used to tell each other,
        nothing hard is ever easy.
If it was, everyone would do it.
Still we must make a choice
        of whether we'll do hard things like go climb Sopris
        or sit at home comfortable, safe, and warm.

I know you would not have retreated
        from life if I had died suddenly
        leaving you to go on without me.
So here I am, a year and a half later,
        putting one foot in front of the other
        and hoping to make you proud.
Even though I am still wondering
        why I am here and you are gone
        and what I need to do
        on this journey home.

Mac McShane
August 25, 2020

Afterword

"Climb the mountain not to plant your flag, but to embrace the challenge, enjoy the air and behold the view. Climb it so you can see the world, not so the world can see you."

David McCullough, Jr.
From his "You Are Not Special" commencement address in 2012

Celebrating Ben – A Life Well-lived

One of the themes in the poetry you just read is the concept of celebration of life. Unless we have been blessed with loving relationships in our lives, we have nothing, literally to lose. The vulnerability and fragility of our existence is precisely due to our connection to those who mean the most to us. For most parents, no relationships are more important in our lives than those with our children and our grandchildren. Yet, we also dare to connect vividly with our partners, our families, and our best friends. As John O'Donohue would label them, they are our Anam Ċara, or soul friends. One way to think about a life well-lived is to consider how many people you touch deeply in your life, or how deeply you have touched those who matter most. At the same time, what matters most to you creates your greatest vulnerability. To love deeply is to knowingly accept the possibility of great loss.

Ben somehow managed to touch many people in his short life. Many I knew, some I had only heard about, and others I did not know at all. My poetry comes out of my attempts at "sense making" about Ben's death and what I need to do to continue putting one foot in front of the other to use his death as a way forward rather than excuse to give up. Theodor Seuss Geisel, Dr.

Seuss to most of us, is often quoted as saying, "When something bad happens you have three choices. You can either let it define you, let it destroy you, or you can let it strengthen you."

I am inspired by how Ben touched so many different people in so many different areas of his life. I ask myself, what am I doing to touch others, connect with others, make a difference in the world? How do I learn to better open my heart, create presence with others, learn to love more fully rather than retreat into myself and the false safety of not taking risks.

We had a celebration of Ben's life less than a week after he died. It was held in Denver, where he grew up even though he had been living in San Francisco for 10 years. Through the haze of my shock and grief, I was struck by the outpouring of love from the five hundred plus people who gathered with us that day as well as the many who were not there and wrote about their sense of loss that Ben was no longer in their lives.

I find comfort in knowing that he did make a difference to so many including myself. I find purpose in wondering how we can all work harder at making a difference. We are alive for a reason, even if it is mostly unknowable to most of us. What will people write about you or me when we are gone? Did it matter that we were here today? Did we make a positive difference in some meaningful way? Can we live more like Ben?

Remembrance of Ben – January 31, 2019

Written and read by Mac McShane

Thank you for being here today to celebrate Ben's life. Ben was an extraordinary human being who touched so many people in profound ways. I could talk about the many amazing aspects of Ben, as could all of you who knew him. We all have great stories that capture the essence of who he was and the people and places and activities that mattered most to him.

I had the privilege of being Ben's father and he taught me as much or more than I taught him. We both cherished our unique bond and the chance to share time together in magical outdoor places and to talk about what was important in our lives. We talked often about our aspirations and our fears. I will forever cherish the weekend we spent together just before he died. Long nights talking about what was most important like being present, doing what we love, learning to be more compassionate towards ourselves, deepening relationships with those who matter most to us, spending time in wild places, and making a difference in the world. In the past year, we both had started to talk more about life being too short and that we could not afford to live as if we were immortal. Instead, we wanted to live with imagination and intention, to live as if there was no time to waste, to love those who mattered most, and to do more of what was most important, even when we did not always know what that meant.

Ben was a master in the art of living as defined by Yvon Chouinard.

> A master in the art of living draws no sharp distinction between his work and his play; his labor and his leisure; his mind and his body; his education and his recreation. He hardly knows which is which. He simply pursues his *vision of excellence* through whatever he is doing, and leaves others to determine whether he is working or playing. To himself, he always appears to be doing both. (Yvon Chouinard, *Let My People Go Surfing: The education of a reluctant businessman.*)

Sometimes people saw Ben as competitive, that he had to win. Yet for him it was less about winning in the sense of being better than someone else and more about "his vision of excellence." They can look the same and both, unfortunately, can, at times, lead to the despondency of feeling that you are mediocre and never good enough at what is most important. They can lead to being too critical, not celebrating success and looking more at what is missing than what is created. But at its best, the "vision of excellence" helps us focus on the process more than the outcome. Ben believed as stated by Yvon Chouinard: "How you climb a mountain is much more important than reaching the top."

Ben was immensely proud of learning to surf and doing it at Ocean Beach off San Francisco, a difficult and constantly changing break. He had no illusions of ever being the best or needing to be. Yet, he found solace there in the challenge of the learning, developing skills, assessing risk, managing fear, building relationships with other surfers, and, most importantly, being in the awesomeness of nature. He was as moved by having a whale breach nearby on a foggy morning with mediocre waves as he was by his recent "best ride ever" of a double overhead wave.

Ben knew, as most of us do, that, as stated by Steve Jobs and many others, "The only certainty in life is death." He would have also liked another quote by Steve Jobs, "If today were the last day of my life, would I want to do what I am about to do today? If the answer is no for too many days in a row – you need to change something."

We will mourn our loss of Ben for as long as we live. I, for one, cannot imagine life without him. Yet, the best homage we can give Ben is to go out and love each other, make a difference in the world, and each pursue our own sense of excellence as we climb our own mountains as best we know how.

I asked Ben, as were skinning up a peak in Aspen days before he died, what he thought was next for him after he developed a fabulously successful hedge fund that gave him and so many others the blessing of financial resources that could buy freedom? His answers were simple, and came out without hesitation, "make a difference in the world, live more simply, find a way to help others, and work to protect the wild places I love." The world is a better place for Ben having lived in it. Thank you for being here to celebrate Ben's life.

Recommended Reading and Listening

Alexander, Eben, *Proof of Heaven: A Neurosurgeon's Journey into the Afterlife* (London, Piatkus, 2012)

Csikszentmihalyi, Mihaly, *Flow: The Psychology of Optimal Experience* (New York, Harper and Row, 1990)

Duckworth, Angela, Grit: *The Power of Passion and Perseverance* (New York, Scribner, 2016)

Duhigg, Charles, *Smarter Faster Better: The Secrets of Being Productive in Life and Business* (New York, Random House, 2016)

Dweck, Carol S., *Mindset: The New Psychology of Success* (New York, Random House, 2006)

Ericsson, Anders and Pool, Robert, *Peak: How All of Us Can Achieve Extraordinary Things* (London, Penguin, Random House, 2016)

Frankl, Viktor, *Man's Search for Meaning* (New York, Pocket Books, 1959)

Fredrickson, Barbara L., *Positivity: Top-Notch Research Reveals the Upward Spiral That Will Change Your Life* (New York, Crown/Random House, 2013)

Haidt, Jonathan, *The Happiness Hypothesis: Finding Modern Truth in Ancient Wisdom* (New York, Basic Books, 2006)

His Holiness the Dalai Lama and Howard Cutler, *The Art of Happiness: A Handbook for Living* (New York: Penguin Putman, 1997)

Housden, Roger, Edited, *Risking Everything: 110 Poems of Love and Revelation* (New York, Harmony Books, 2003)

Hutchinson, Alex, *Endure: Mind, Body, and the Curiously Elastic Limits of Human Performance* (New York, Harper Collins, 2018)

Kabat-Zinn, Jon, *Wherever You Go, There You Are: Mindfulness Meditation in Everyday Life* (New York, Hyperion, 1994)

Kalanithi, Paul, *When Breath Becomes Air* (New York, Random House, 2016)

Kornfield, Jack, *The Wise Heart: A Guide to the Universal Teachings of Buddhist Psychology* (New York, Bantam Dell, 2008)

Mumford, George, *The Mindful Athlete: Secrets to Pure Performance* (Berkley, Parallax Press, 2015)

Nepo, Mark, *The Book of Awakening: Having the Life You Want by Being Present to the Life You Have* (San Francisco, Conari Press, 2011)

O'Connor, M.R., *Wayfinding: The Science and Mystery of How Humans Navigate the World* (New York, St. Martin's Press, 2019)

O'Donohue, John, *Anam Ċara: A Book of Celtic Wisdom* (New York: Harper Perennial, 1997)

O'Donohue, John, *Longing and Belonging: The Complete John O'Donohue* Audio Collection (Boulder, Sounds True, 2012)

Sanberg, Sheryl and Grant, Adam, *Option B: Facing Adversity, Building Resilience and Finding Joy* (New York, Alfred Knopf, 2017)

Siegel, Daniel, *Aware: The Science and Practice of Presence* (New York, Penguin Random House, 2018)

Walters, Dorothy, *The Ley Lines of the Soul: Poems of Ecstasy and Ascension* (Boulder, Xlibris, 2012)

Watkins, Alan, *Coherence: The Secret Science of Brilliant Leadership* (London, Kogan Page Limited, 2014)

Wilber, Ken, *Kosmic Consciousness* (Boulder, Sounds True, 2003)

Zimmermann, Susan, *Writing to Heal the Soul: Transforming Grief and Loss Through Writing* (New York, Three Rivers Press, 2002)

Acknowledgements

I did not set out to write a book, only to survive the loss of my son, Ben, at 35 in a horrific backcountry ski accident. This book would not have been possible without the tender love and encouragement of Cynthia Calvin, my wife for 30 years and my partner in raising Ben for 33 years. As my journal writings somehow morphed into poems, I began reading what I had written to Cynthia in mornings over tea and coffee. Devastated by her own grief and disbelief, she, better than anyone, understood my own grief and work to both honor the memory of Ben and stay afloat. She encouraged me to share my writing with friends and family and, over time, the concept of this book emerged as a way to share my inner world with others and to better understand how not to give in to nihilism, despondency, and despair. Ben's life was enhanced by his relationship with Cynthia and I am very blessed to have such a great partner in my life.

In addition, I am grateful beyond words for the friends, family, and colleagues who have encouraged me, supported me, grieved with me, and continued to work and play with me. Thank you for staying connected with me on this strange and mysterious journey we call life. I will not try to list by name all the people who have so generously lifted me up, reminded me of the ways Ben touched so many people, and continue to give meaning to my life. Thank you also to the large number of friends and family who came on such short notice to Ben's memorial service the week he died and who helped me understand how much he had meant to so many whose lives he touched. Your presence kept me going when I did not think it would be possible.

I particularly want to mention my sister, Marilyn McShane Levine, and my nephew, Josh Levine, who have stayed in close contact during this time, making up for some of the crater left in my life by Ben's absence. They both had their own special relationships with Ben and know firsthand the tremendous hole left in all of our lives by his death. Thank you.

The book you have in your hand or on some device, has the look and feel of a real book due to the efforts of my designer, Cindi Yaklich, who patiently worked to bring my rough concepts of what this book should look like into a much better emotional and visual experience.

Lastly, I want to thank my amazing editor, Lynn Wagner. Recommended to me by my friend and her fellow writing coach, Shari Caudron, Lynn bravely took on what must have sounded like an impossible task of editing the poetry and prose of some guy she had never met, who had never written poetry before and now wanted to publish his book about the loss of his beloved son. Thank you, Lynn, for the courage to accept the task and more importantly for building the trusting partnership with me that allowed us to transform this book from a dream into a reality. Both the book and I are better for your thoughtful work.

About the Author

Mac McShane lives, works, and plays in the mountains around Aspen in a house that he and his wife Cynthia built looking out at magical high peaks in the Roaring Fork Valley. He was born on the coast of Connecticut and gradually travelled across the US attending various universities along the way. He earned an undergraduate engineering degree in Naval Architecture and Marine Engineering from the University of Michigan, a Masters of Education degree in Community Education from the University of Massachusetts, and a Doctorate in Psychology from the University of Denver. He had careers in submarine and hovercraft design as a Naval Architect, a leader of adolescent mountaineering trips, a teacher at the high school and college level, a clinical psychologist working with adults and children, and a child custody evaluator among other things. Drawn to questions of "why is it so hard for humans to continue to grow and change?" and "what does it mean to have a life well-lived?" Mac moved from clinical and consulting psychology into Leadership Development and Executive Coaching. He is an International Coaching Federation (ICF) certified coach who works with various companies and individuals in both government and private enterprise throughout the US and globally. When his only son Ben was killed in a tragic backcountry ski accident, Mac turned to writing as a way to both survive and search for a path forward. He shares his journey here through prose and poetry, hoping it will help others dealing with tragedy and loss and inspire us all to continue developing into the best we can be in this time of turmoil and division. Together we can make a difference.